Gamify your life

Crush those clueless criticisms   44

Six steps to streaming success   46

Flex those fingers   48

Dealing with downtime   50

How to cosplay   52

Video games versus...   54

Don't let trolls drag you down   56

Could you be an esports champion?   58

How to get a job in games   60

You know you've played too
    many video games when...   62

PUBLISHER'S NOTE

The exercises and activities in this book have been checked by an
exercise consultant but all participants in such activities must assume
responsibility for their own actions and safety. If you have any health
problems or medical conditions, consult with your physician before
undertaking any of the activities. The information and advice contained in
this guide book cannot replace sound judgement and good decision
making, nor does the scope of this book allow for disclosure of all the
potential hazards and risks involved in the activities herein.

A brief history of video games

Fast-forward through 40+ years of classics and controversies.

70s

Say hello to *Pong*, the first arcade machine. People play it so much it breaks down!

Gaming comes home as the Atari 2600 kicks off the first console craze.

Mario, Nintendo's mustachioed plumber, makes his first appearance in *Donkey Kong*.

80s

The *Space Invaders* arcade machine is so popular in Japan there's a shortage of 100-yen coins.

A flood of bad games reportedly leads Atari to bury unsold cartridges in the New Mexico desert.

The Nintendo GameBoy becomes the first smash-hit handheld console, selling almost 120 million units.

90s

Video games go from geeky to mainstream with the launch of the Sony PlayStation.

Microsoft's Xbox becomes the first serious challenger to the PlayStation.

Games truly go mobile with the likes of *Angry Birds* and *Candy Crush*. Now everyone's playing!

Music games such as *Rock Band* use mics, guitars and drums instead of normal controllers.

Politicians and pressure groups try to get *Mortal Kombat* banned because of its violence and gore!

Sega's *Sonic the Hedgehog* speeds into action, sparking years of Sega/Nintendo rivalry.

The *Minecraft* craze sees sales of the game top 122 million in seven years.

Smart devices and social games let you play with anyone, anywhere!

The ideal gaming set-up

A screen and a seat don't make a games den.

Choose the right room

In an age of VR headsets and motion controllers, it's important to pick a game space with room to move. Even traditional games call for stretching and screen breaks, so think big from the start.

Don't skimp on screens

Why opt for a single screen when you've already set up a supersized games room? Make the most of a generous space with three linked-up monitors for extra-widescreen gaming.

Get a gear rack

Build or buy a rack for your controllers, chargers, headphones and other kit. You are a gaming ninja and this is your armoury. Treat it with respect and keep it within easy reach at all times.

Set the mood

A good games den isn't just a room: it's a shrine to all that makes gaming great. Decorate your space with memorabilia – from retro carts to convention passes and collectable figures. Even add a display cabinet!

Stock up on snacks

Add a mini fridge to your gaming area to grab cold drinks and snacks without pressing pause. Kitchen trips are for suckers – unless you move your games den to the kitchen, of course.

Get your games in order

There's nothing worse than not being able to find a game when you need it most. Keep them all in one place, in their boxes, and ideally in alphabetical order. It makes sense and it looks cool.

Snack battles

Find the right fuel for your game night.

Pizza

Everyone loves pizza, but all that cheese will make you pile on the pounds like *Streetfighter 2*'s E Honda at an all-you-can-eat buffet. One slice is fine, but you need to hundred-hand-slap the rest back into the box.

Cookies

Have you seen where all those crumbs go? They pile up in your keyboard and start to attract small mammals. If you don't want keys that crunch like the bottom of a hamster cage, step away from the cookie jar.

Sweets

Choose candy for your fuel and you might as well bid farewell to your teeth. And how will that play when you're live-streaming to your adoring fans? You'll look ridiculous and no one will understand what you're saying.

Sushi

Sushi is a national dish in Japan, the country that also gave us the fighting art of Judo. That doesn't mean eating fish rolls will make you into a master judoka, but if it doesn't... well, you've still enjoyed some sushi.

PLAYER 2

Muesli bar

Oats, nuts and fruit are great for slow-release energy, which is just what you need for a long gaming session. If only there was a food that smooshed them all together in a delicious block of sticky goo. Oh, hello, muesli bar.

PLAYER 4

Frozen grapes

All the satisfying sweetness of candy, without the tooth-rotting risks that make you look like you've gone five rounds with *Streetfighter*'s Chun Li. Also good for flick-it-up-and-catch-it-in-your-mouth victory moves.

PLAYER 6

Engage maximum comfort levels

Get the details right to set yourself up for gaming success.

1

Screens

Modern screens can cope with millions of colours, but you lose some shades if you sit at an angle. Position yourself directly in front, at a distance of about 7ft (2.1m) for a 60in (152cm) screen.

2

Headphones

Over-ear cans are a must for immersive audio. Don't crank them up high – just play with the bass for a fuller sound.

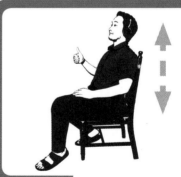

3

Seating

No slouching on the couch when there's serious gaming to be done! Sit upright in a straight-backed chair to maximise your alertness.

5

Surroundings

Game time is your time. Keep the wider world at bay by muting your phone, switching off social media, drawing the curtains and closing all the doors. Locking them is optional.

RING! RING!

4

Controllers

Always charge your controllers between sessions to beat the curse of "Batteries Low". Keep all your cables tidy, too – unless you like knot-based puzzle games.

6

Company

Choose your gaming company wisely. A pet makes an ideal companion if you don't want to be distracted by human small talk.

OLD SCHOOL

Armed and ready

Think of the controller as an extension of your arms. Let's exercise them.

EASY

Console curls

You can't do this with a slim console. Dig out a heavy first-generation Xbox or PlayStation 4. Stand upright with the console in two hands, bend your arms at the elbow and lift the console towards your chin. Keep your upper arms flat to your sides to work your biceps. Hold for a second, release and repeat.

MEDIUM

Controller jabs and hooks

Hold a controller in each hand and mimic the moves of a boxer. Be sure to keep a firm hold of the controllers so you don't fling them out of a window as you swing jabs, crosses, hooks and uppercuts at your imaginary opponent. If you do, going outside to track them down can be considered part of your exercise plan.

HARDCORE

The precarious plank

This one's all about core strength training. It's also about not dropping your precariously placed console. Stretch out in the plank position: face the floor, and balance on your toes and the lower part of your arms. Ask someone to place a console just below your shoulders. Now try extending one arm at a time out in front of you without losing your console.

Hold a console in two hands

Bend arms at the elbow

Squeeze the console towards you

Grab a controller and assume a boxer pose

Swing a left cross with the hand holding the controller

Throw a left hook, too

Lie in the plank position

Still in the plank, extend one arm at a time

Don't go bug-eyed!

Screen time making your eyes itch? Be sure to protect your peepers...

Use the 20-20-20 rule

Every 20 minutes, look away from the screen at a distance of at least 20ft (6m), for 20 seconds or more. It's an easy-to-remember way to get a decent screen break during games.

Wear shades outside

A sudden change from screen light to daylight takes a toll on your eyes, so stick on your sunnies if you go outside straight after gaming. It'll also make you look cool.

Take regular VR breaks

Virtual-reality headsets convince your brain you're seeing depth, but really everything is happening very close to your eyes. Take frequent sit-down breaks to combat disorientation and eye strain.

Eat a feast for your eyes

Your diet affects your eyes just as it does the rest of your body. Foods associated with healthy eyes include dark leafy greens like kale and spinach, and oily fish such as tuna and salmon.

Keep your lenses clean

If you wear glasses or contact lenses, clean them regularly to avoid eye infections. Don't share VR headsets before cleaning them, either. Who knows what's in your best mate's eyes!

Take a break before bed

Bright screens block the chemicals your brain uses to help you sleep. Stop gaming an hour before you turn in and spend the time doing something else like reading – about games, obv.

17

A perfect gaming day

Don't waste a moment with this round-the-clock guide.

7AM Wake, brush teeth, then start the day with a puzzle app on your smartphone. It'll get your brain in gear for the day ahead.

8AM Fuel up! An energy-packed breakfast will get you through the morning.

9AM Morning session: get fully immersed with an intense roleplaying game or first-person shooter. Allow no distractions!

1PM Grab a light lunch and go outside. The air will freshen your mind (and clothes) for the afternoon.

2PM Afternoon session: slow the pace with an open-world or survival game. Take time to explore the unknown and your own creativity.

6PM

Take a power break with some exercise and a decent meal. A few stretches and a protein fix will set you up for an evening online with other gamers.

7PM

Further break the gaming bubble and reluctantly re-enter the real world, just for a while. Listen to tunes, a podcast or read the latest headlines.

8PM

Evening session: this one's all about the multiplayer action. Play competitive sport sims and co-op games with friends online.

12AM

Time to power down. For the best night's recharge, take a 30-minute screen break before you turn in.

7AM

Wake, brush teeth... And do it all again!

A home heptathlon

Exercises to stop you seizing up during long gaming sessions.

1

Star jumps

Collect seven stars in a Super Mario game and you're invincible. Find out if seven star jumps work the same way.

2

Rocket jumps

Squat down then power into the air, landing softly to use the momentum to repeat. Feel the burn.

3

"Soft put"

Shot put with a sofa cushion. Draw back a cushion in one hand and throw it. It's both exercise *and* stress relief.

4

Sofa sprints

Do a set of high-intensity sprints across your living room, avoiding any pet hurdles.

5

Broom javelin

Go outside, grab a broom and throw it javelin-style. Just make sure it lands in open space!

Long jump

Stay outside for this one. Swing your arms and imagine you're leaping across a chasm.

6

Stair climbing

Sprint up and down stairs for 90 seconds for a high-intensity leg session that works out any last couch kinks.

7

Who's gaming when?

These are the players you'll meet online at different times of day.

8.00pm

Tired parents come out to play. Marriages are saved and strained in equal measure.

6.00pm

The competitive online gamer settles in for another big multiplayer night right about now.

4.00pm

It's kids o'clock just as soon as school's out. Are you *sure* that's homework?

Midnight

Got to be up early tomorrow, but there's probably time for just one more go...

3.00am

It could be 3.00am or 3.00pm. These players have lost all concept of time and space.

Midday

Say hello to the lunchbreak gamers, getting a cheeky half hour in between sales meetings.

5.00am

Go easy on the exhausted players at the end an all-night session.

Indoor leg exercises

Keep fit without putting down your console or controller.

EASY

Straight leg raises

Want to work out without breaking a sweat? This is one exercise you can do without even getting off your backside. Just lie on the floor, raise one leg, and hold it straight for a second before lowering slowly. Repeat with the other leg, then alternate. After a while, you won't even notice you're doing it.

MEDIUM

Sideways bicycle kicks

Try actual cycling while gaming and you'll end up in hospital. But ride an invisible bike as you play and you can work out without wheels! Lie on your side and cycle your top leg 20 times before shifting onto your other side and repeating. Keep going until you get an imaginary flat tyre.

HARDCORE

Squats

Looking for a bigger challenge? Try gaming on your feet, with frequent half-squats. Stand with your feet shoulder-width apart, bend your knees and push your hips forward. Hold the position for a second, then rise back to standing. Keep it up in regular sessions and you'll be doing flying dragon kicks in no time.

Lie with your legs outstretched

Raise and hold each leg in turn

Lie on your side and work your top leg

Swap sides and repeat

Stand with your legs apart and your back upright

Bend your legs while keeping your back straight

How to find new gaming friends

Sure, you've got plenty of pals, but it's always good to have more!

Join Looking For Groups

Looking For Groups (LFGs) are useful online communities of gamers who are looking to play with people of a similar ability and want to make new, like-minded friends.

Play co-op, not competitive

Yes it's fun to win, but nothing puts people off playing more than being endlessly beaten. Play co-op games and you can coach those with less experience, rather than trounce them every time.

Keep it regular

Once you've made friends online, arrange a regular weekly time to play together and stick to it. As soon as it becomes an event, everyone will look forward to it and be more likely to commit.

Tackle things as a team

If you're making maps and levels in a game like *Minecraft*, it's a lot easier with extra hands. Try teaming up with lots of players in one lobby to make a masterpiece – and some new friends!

Make a movie

Lots of games have built-in tools for making mini-movies. Make friends by recruiting other players to star in your short films, then be sure to include all their screen names in your closing credits.

Get social

Post ads on social media and forums, describing yourself and what you look for in other players. You'll be surprised how many like-minded gamers are looking for someone just like you.

4-D_WANDERER

COZMIC_BOHO

DANDYMAN

TEETH-N-CURLZ

27

Be the host with the most

Six essentials for an awesome gaming party.

Games

Variety is the spice of life, so make sure there are lots of different games to play, and that none get played for more than one hour.

Snacks

Theme all the snacks and drinks around characters and items from the games you're playing. Save some of the best as rewards for top players.

Prizes

Keep scores and give prizes, but not just for games skill. Give awards for being a good sport, for funny fails and for helping other players.

5

Nerfs

Level the playing field with real-life nerfs. Make the best players play one-handed or, even better, operate the controller with their feet.

GameSpeak:
A nerf reduces a character's power or skill in a game.

4

Forfeits

Call out unsporting behaviour with fun forfeits. Bad losers should take a soy sauce shot or chow down on a raw chilli.

A big finish

At the end of the night, have a ceremony for whoever tops the leaderboard. This lucky player gets to host the party next time!

6

29

Gaming mindfulness

Become one with the games and the games will become one with you...

Slow down

Pick a level you know and play it again slowly. Appreciate the details and you might find hidden extras.

Step back

Always stuck on the same level? Take a deep breath and look around. There may be something you've missed.

Feel the vibrations
Focus on physical feedback from your controller. It could be a hint to nudge you in the right direction.

Embrace the now
Take each task as it comes. Explore everything you see before you move on, rather than racing to finish.

What kind of gamer are you?

Take the test and find out…

WHAT'S MOST IMPORTANT TO YOU WHEN YOU CREATE A CHARACTER?

A Striking fear into the hearts of my enemies
B Looking cool and colourful
C Tooling up with weapons and gear

WHAT ARE YOUR FAVOURITE IN-GAME WEAPONS?

A Big, loud rocket launchers
B Tranquiliser darts
C Sniper rifles

WHEN DO YOU STOP PLAYING A GAME?

A If I'm bored, I hit the off switch
B When my friends move on to something else
C Once I've completed every mission

HOW DO YOU FEEL ABOUT COLLECTING THINGS IN GAMES?

A If it makes me tougher, I'm all for it
B Gotta get everything, no matter where it is!
C Life's too short to track down 100 feathers

HOW OFTEN DO YOU PLAY GAMES WITH OTHERS?

A All the time – the more victims the better!
B Often – isn't that the point of gaming?
C There are too many trolls, so I prefer to go solo

HOW IMPORTANT IS A GAME'S STORY?

A Whatever, dude. I'm here for the action
B I create my own stories when I play
C I want full immersion in another world

NOW CHECK YOUR RESULTS!

WHAT'S MOST IMPORTANT WHEN PLAYING WITH OTHERS?

A Winning, obviously
B Fair play and teamwork
C I don't play well with others

WHAT'S THE BEST THING ABOUT GAMING?

A The adrenaline rush of action
B Having a laugh with my friends
C Solving really tough challenges

WHAT'S MOST IMPORTANT IN A VIRTUAL WORLD?

A Making my mark on the landscape
B Finding secrets in every single corner
C Keeping my hoard of gold away from others

If you answered...

Mostly As:
You're a hardcore gamer. You're here to win, gloat about it, and then do it all again. And if you die while kicking butt, you'll leave a good-looking avatar, right?

Mostly Bs:
You're a social gamer. More players equals more fun in your world, especially when you're all on the same side, solving problems and exploring together.

Mostly Cs:
You're a solo gamer. Gaming is your escape from other people, and a chance to get lost in different worlds – ideally for weeks at a time!

Shooter

Shoot'em-ups are all about a 30-second loop of action. Running and gunning, throwing yourself around, juggling weapons until they run dry and tossing grenades into every corner. Subtlety is not part of your arsenal.

Horror

With non-stop scares, the only way to win is to overcome your fears. If that means embracing the horror and sinking to the level of your monstrous enemies… Well, you're pushed to extremes, so what else can you do?

RPG

Role-playing games let you spend hours building a character before recruiting other players and setting off on epic quests, many of which go on for weeks. You practically live the game, and the real world is just an irritation.

Stealth

Stealth games are the opposite of shooters. You still get the thrill of taking down an enemy, but you need to plan and work for it. Hugging walls, moving silently... Patience is just as important as the weapon in your hands.

PLAYER 2

Survival

A whole different kind of hell, survival sims force you to live on the edge. Micro-managing is the only way to keep breathing when every scrap of food is a luxury and a tiny problem can quickly spiral into disaster.

PLAYER 4

MOBA

Where RPGs can be an endless quest, Multiplayer Online Battle Arenas offer the quick thrill of one pre-set character in a brutal skirmish against an enemy base. They're all about quick reactions and in-the-moment strategy.

PLAYER 6

Gaming yoga

Hunched over from playing too many games? Try these yoga moves.

EASY

LEVEL 1

The Seated Twist: you're a thief, sitting on top of a horde of treasure, stretching.

Sit on the floor with your legs out in front of you. Cross your left foot over the right thigh and bend your left knee. Keep your right knee pointing to the ceiling. Place your right elbow on the outside of your left knee, and your left hand on the floor behind you. Twist to the left as far as comfortable and keep both bum cheeks on the floor. Hold that pose for one minute, then switch sides and repeat.

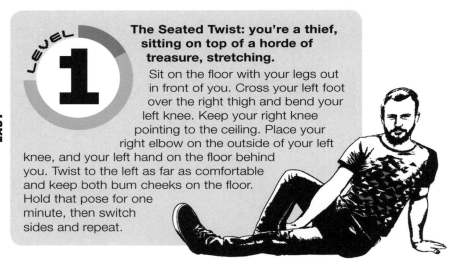

MEDIUM

LEVEL 2

The Warrior: you are a ninja, poised and ready to defend or attack in an instant.

Stand with your legs 3–4ft (1m) apart, turn the right foot 90 degrees outwards and the left foot in slightly. Extend out your arms with your palms down. Relax those shoulders! Bend your right knee 90 degrees, making sure the knee remains over the right ankle. Look out over your right hand and hold the position for one minute. Now switch sides and repeat.

The Tree: avoid conflict by blending in with the world around you.

Stand with both arms down at your sides. Move your weight onto your left foot and place the sole of your right foot on the inside thigh of your left leg. Keep your hips facing forward. When comfortable with your balance, bring your hands together in front of you in a prayer position. Inhale and raise your arms above your shoulders, with palms facing each other. Hold that position for 30 seconds, then lower your arms and repeat on the other leg.

LEVEL 3

HARDCORE

The Self Hug: fighter, assassin or commander, we all need to give ourselves a hug when virtual life gets tough.

Lie flat on your back on the floor or the sofa and bend both legs. Place your hands on the back of your thighs and draw your legs up towards your chest. Breathe deeply, squeezing your legs closer to your chest as you exhale. Close your eyes and let out a little sigh. Keep hugging. Hug a little bit more. Relax. Have a little nap. You deserve it.

LEVEL 0

RELAXED

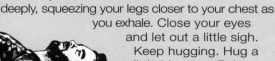

37

Dress like a hero

Take style tips from game characters to survive a day at the shops.

1 The Explorer

Perfect for checking out second-hand shops – digging for dusty old retro games and long-forgotten consoles.

3 The Fighter

Swoop in and grab the last copy of the latest hit in some loose-fitting leisurewear.

2 The Survivor

Equip yourself for any weather when you're braving the line at a midnight game launch.

Midnight game launch

The Driver

When the sales are on, make like a car and swerve through the crowds on rollerblades.

The Soldier

Who needs carrier bags when you've got combat trousers and a giant rucksack?

The Technomage

Make buying games online more fun by dressing as a wizard in your own home.

Get more bang for your buck

Gaming doesn't have to be expensive. Spend wisely and reap the rewards.

Share with friends

Regular games swaps with your mates don't just save you money – they are also a great way to pick up hints and tips, and pass on some wisdom of your own.

Find the freebies

There are loads of free games available online, and some of them are actually really good. Just watch out for in-game charges for extra content, time or buffs.

Stream your sessions

Live-streaming your games for other people to watch can make you money on sites like Twitch. Be entertaining and you could build up a lucrative following!

Become a beta tester

Sign up to take part in beta tests and you can play games for free before they're released. You just have to put up with any bugs the designers haven't fixed yet.

Sell your old games

Games you've finished look good on the shelf, but cash looks better in your wallet. You can also trade in games in many stores for money off other pre-owned titles.

Pre-order new ones

Committing to games at pre-release rates guards against price rises, and many sellers will match any price drops, too. There may also be bonus in-game content.

GameSpeak:
A buff is a short-term or permanent increase in a character's skills.

Gamify your life

Reality sucks! Give yourself points for getting through the day.

Get out of bed, brush teeth
(5-point freshness bonus for flossing)

+5 points

Eat a healthy breakfast
(5-point bonus if it includes some fruit)

+5 points

Take out the trash
(5-point penalty for spillage)

+10 points

Cupcake reward at 50 points

Compliment a stranger
(10-point blush bonus if they compliment you back)

+5 points

Get to work/school on time
(5-point smugness bonus if early)

+10 points

Donate to charity
(5-point bonus if donating a great game)

+20 points

Buy someone coffee
(Coffee bonus for you too if you already know their order)

+5 points

Drink a healthy drink
(5-point bonus if you juice your own fruit)

+5 points

Host a games night
(10-point good-sport bonus for letting your friends win)

+25 points

Tot up your score before bed
(Midnight snack bonus if it's a new high score)

+10 points

Pizza reward at 100 points

YOU WIN AT LIFE!

Go to the gym
(10-point feel-the-burn bonus for trying new equipment)

+10 points

43

Crush those clueless criticisms

*If someone snipes that games are bad for you,
hit back with these forceful facts.*

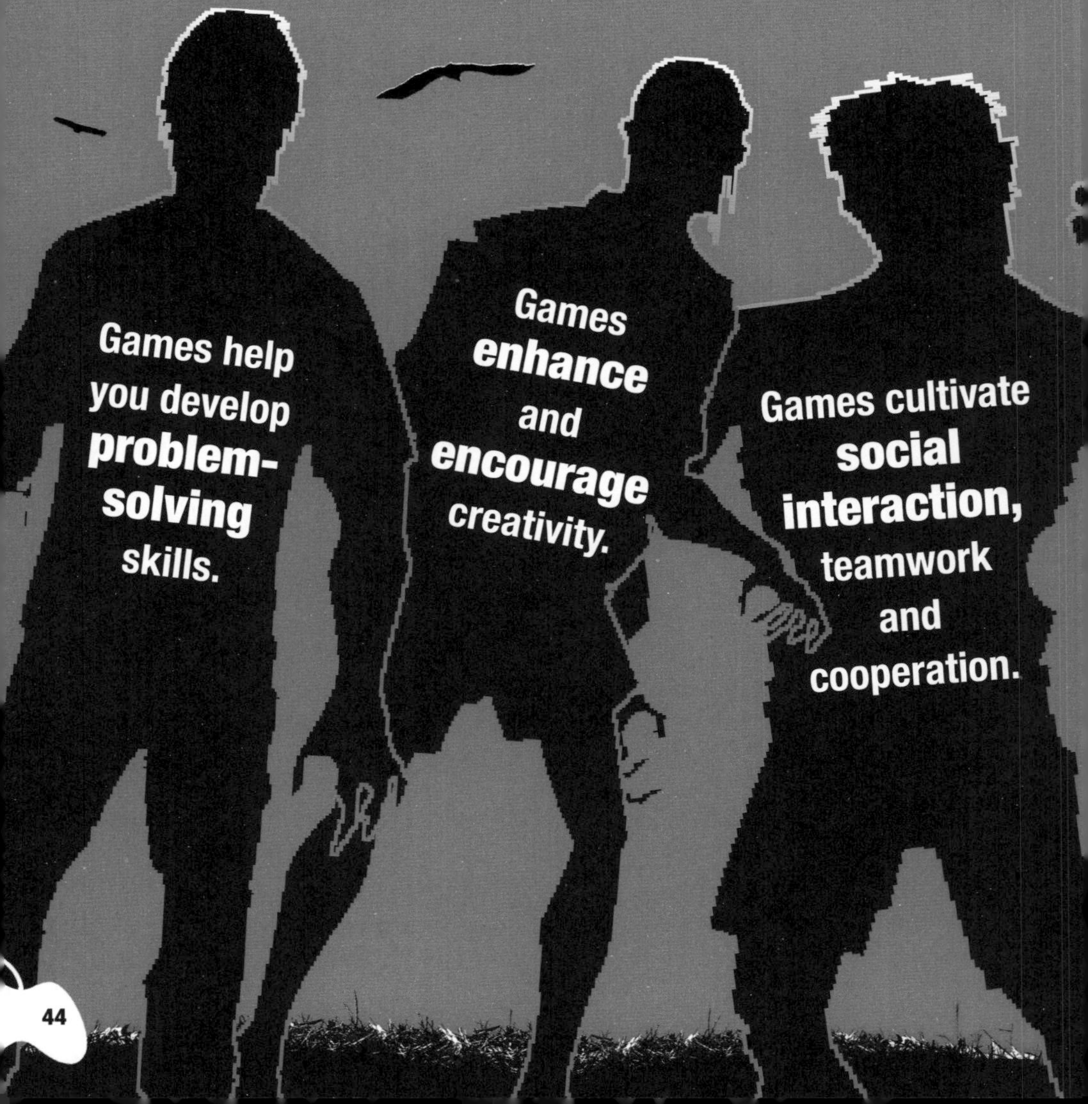

Games help
you develop
**problem-
solving**
skills.

Games
enhance
and
encourage
creativity.

Games cultivate
**social
interaction,**
teamwork
and
cooperation.

Games improve your **reflexes, hand-eye coordination** and **quick-thinking** skills.

Games teach **pattern** recognition.

Games **relieve anxiety** and help you to **relax.**

Six steps to streaming success

Don't just play games – stream your sessions and build your own fanbase.

Get the right kit

You don't need to spend a fortune, but the better your kit, the better your stream. Get yourself a decent microphone with no hiss, and a camera that won't make you into a mess of pixels.

Keep talking

Your fans want to hear from you as much as they want to see the game itself. Vocalise all your reactions to the game, get a dialogue going with viewers and be sure to welcome noobs.

Find your niche

Anyone can stream, so what makes you different? Look for a gap in the market, then make it your thing. Maybe it will be the type of game you play, or how you involve your viewers in the game.

Be consistent

Think of your stream like a TV show. Pick a weekly slot when you will be online and plug it on social media. Give your stream a title and always use it. All this will help to build viewers and familiarity.

Involve viewers

People watch streams to be a part of something. Give viewers lots of ways to interact, like chances to have characters in your games named after them. Everyone likes to see their name on screen.

Enjoy it

Streaming won't make you rich and famous. A few lucky people make a living from it, but fun has to be the main reason to do it. You play games anyway, so why not share the fun with others?

Flex those fingers

It's fastest fingers first in many games, so don't neglect your digital dexterity.

EASY

Claw stretch

Hold your hand out in front of you, palm upright. Flex your fingertips and thumb into the palm to form a claw. Hold for 30 seconds then repeat, switching hands. For extra resistance, hold a soft ball in your palm as you form the claw. For more entertainment value, pursue young relatives with your monster mitts.

MEDIUM

Thumb touches

Hold your hand up in front of you with your fingers and thumb outstretched. Then touch each fingertip in turn to your thumb tip, forming a series of "O" shapes for 30 seconds each. Finish by touching both middle fingers to your thumb at once, just for the fun of making gnarly devil horns. Now repeat on the other hand.

HARDCORE

Thumb extensions

Not a way to grow extra-long thumbs (though that would be cool), this is in fact another tension exercise that works the opposite way to squeezing a ball. Fit an elastic band snugly around the fingers and thumb on one hand, then slowly extend your thumb as far from your fingers as you can. Hold for 30 seconds, then repeat.

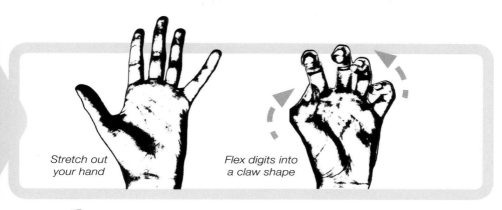

Stretch out
your hand

Flex digits into
a claw shape

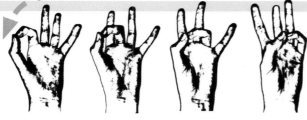
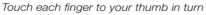

Touch each finger to your thumb in turn

Form devil horns with
two fingers and thumb

Place an elastic band
around your hand

Extend your thumb
and fingers

49

Dealing with downtime

It's not the end of the world if your game goes offline.

Embrace it

1 Downtime can be the universe's way of telling you to take a break. Walk away, enjoy something else, then come back bright and eager.

OFF
(and on again)

Reboot it

2 Turn your machine off and on again. This age-old advice really does solve 90 per cent of downtime disasters. Heed the wisdom of the ancients.

Accept it

3 Stay calm. Things break all the time. You can either be offline and cool with it, or offline and angry. Rage won't get your game back faster.

Talk about it

If it's just the game that's down, get on forums or social media and talk tactics with other offline players.

MARK_PF_379

LAURA_123

Imagine it

Be the game! Replay tricky scenarios in your head while you wait for the real thing to return.

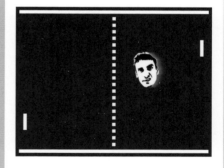

Celebrate it

If the game's down while it's performing an update, remember that without regular revisions we'd all still be playing *Pong*!

How to cosplay

Nothing says "I love gaming" like dressing as your favourite character.

Think creatively

If you can't settle on a favourite character, mix it up to make your own mash-up of characters and genres. How about a *Minecraft* Mario, Lara Croft the Hedgehog or a steampunk Princess Zelda?

Be inspired

Go to conventions and other events to meet cosplayers and ask them about their costumes. Compliment people on their look before fishing for tips and you might even make new friends!

Put pen to paper

Sketch out your idea before you buy or make anything. Even if you've got a concept in your head, a few doodles will spark new ideas for details and customisation – even if you can't draw!

Be realistic

Your finished look can be as outlandish as you like, but keep it real when it comes to time and budget. Better to complete a simple outfit than end up abandoning something too ambitious.

Take a test drive

Try out your costume before attending an event to make sure it will be comfortable all day and won't fall apart on the move. Ask a gaming friend if you look like who you're supposed to, too!

Be confident

What will make your costume a success is the confidence with which you project your alter ego. Copy your character's poses and mannerisms and embrace being someone different for a day.

MMORPGs

Massively multiplayer online role-playing games let you play with hundreds of people at once. There are hundreds of hours of adventure to be had, and you can build your perfect character over several years of play.

Extreme sports games

All the thrill of live sport but with no risk of permanent physical injury. Sure, there's no actual exercise involved, but when it's a fine line between getting fit and getting flattened, it can be in your interest to stay in the virtual skate park.

Action games

The minute-to-minute thrill of an action game is hard to beat. Movement, exploration and combat go hand in hand, and call for lightning reactions as the game throws endless problems and bad guys in your path.

Pen-and-paper RPGs

All the graphics are in your head, dude. Your playing buddies are few, but they are all in the same room as you, and the imagination of a good Dungeon Master is all you need to create never-ending adventures, quests and dangers.

PLAYER 2

Skateboarding

Replace finger tricks with the real thing and you'll get a major buzz from shredding the streets. It's easy to get started and you see everyday objects in a new way, as street furniture turns into obstacles and challenges.

PLAYER 4

Board games

Though not action-packed, lots of board games call for quick thinking, too. Video games such as *Doom*, *Fallout* and *Dark Souls* have all been adapted into board games, and come with brilliant little character tokens, too!

PLAYER 6

Don't let trolls drag you down

A handful of gamers are out to spoil it for the rest, but they can be beaten.

Hit the mute button

Mute anyone being rude or troublesome to you or your friends. The loudest trolls are only looking for a reaction, so when they realise you're ignoring them they will get bored and go away.

Hit the report button

Don't be afraid to report bad behaviour. Most online platforms have systems in place to tackle trolls, and using them makes it harder for your tormentors to target others in future.

Don't sink to their level

Everyone gets upset or angry sometimes, but throwing insults of your own will only escalate the problem. If a troll sees that you are easy to enrage, they will keep on coming back for more.

Do what you came to do

You came online to play, so play! Don't allow yourself to be banished by bad manners. Let your game skills do the talking and be the better person by winning fairly and squarely.

Surround yourself with friends

Trolls are just a vocal minority. Remind yourself of that by playing with good friends and setting out to make new ones. Make sure everyone knows that they need to be nice to stay in the group.

Be a role model for others

Gaming doesn't have to be competitive. Team up with others in co-operative games and coach new players. Then ask them to do the same in future to foster good community spirit.

GameSpeak:
A troll is an online bully who sets out to cause trouble.

H8TER

57

Could you be an esports champion?

Think you've got what it takes to play professionally?
It's a lot tougher than it looks...

TRAINING

Just like playing traditional sports at a professional level, esports require hard work and dedication – practising for at least 10 hours a day. Gaming all day might sound cool, but it could also suck the fun out of your favourite thing.

PLAYING

Professional esports players live together 24 hours a day. It's a hotbox environment, with your coach on hand at all times, too. Could you cope with eating, sleeping and unwinding under the same roof as your fellow players?

WINNING

The prize pots might be big, but they get split between all the players on a team, as well as their manager, their coach and others. Rather than being life-changing, the rewards are best seen as a bonus on top of a professional player's wage.

BRANDING

For many players, the big money comes from merchandise and sponsorship deals. Representing brands will get you lots of free stuff, but it also means being on your best behaviour at all times. You're a role model now. Don't let the fame go to your head!

How to get a job in games

Make games pay with six ways to break into the video games industry.

Sign up for QA testing

Games developers use quality-assurance testers to get feedback on games in development. Look up your nearest developer and drop them a line. It could be your first step on the career ladder.

Build something cool

Use in-game tools and creative games like *Minecraft* to build levels, characters, logos and more. Share them online wherever you can to catch the eye of professionals looking for new blood.

Join mod communities

Modding communities share tweaks they have made to existing games. They often have professional developers among their members, making them a great place to get your talents spotted.

Enter local game jams

Game jams are events where small teams work to create a game. They are often attended by game developers who give advice (and free food!), making them a great place to make industry contacts.

Set up an online CV

Whether it's a YouTube showreel or a simple blog, an up-to-date online list of your achievements is a quick and clear way to share your interests, skills and talents with potential employers.

Do a development course

Universities offer game development courses covering coding, marketing, art and more. You'll need maths and problem-solving skills, but who wouldn't want to be a game-studying student?

You know you've played too many video games when...

Or, video game logic doesn't work so well in the real world.

1 You try stuffing 50 different items in your backpack.

2 You expect to hear the achievement unlocked sound after completing an exam paper.

3 You walk into a stranger's house and rummage through their cupboards.

62